CONTENTS

Entrance

I wait in the wings upstage left,
breathe in through the nose,
out through the mouth, cluck
consonants, throw forth some vowels.

Is my first move down or right?
In which pocket did I put the ring?
Did I pick up the ring?
Is this the scene with the ring?

When will my skin begin to pucker
like Cheddar Gorge, bones tinkle
like pockets full of seashells,
ears fill with ocean gurgles,
head brim with jibber jabber,
memory bound like a puppy,
vomit, piss and shit pour out
with no discernible warning?

I straighten my waistcoat,
hope they laugh tonight,
and stride into light.

Pursued by Well-being

It's like seeing sheep in the high street,
or molten gold hanging from the trees.

It's like hearing sand forming on a wave,
or picking fruit in a stone-damp cave.

It has feet that move like wheels on fire,
and tastes of coal-blue blood and desire.

It's the scent of snipe you smell at the cross
that makes you look up to the tip of the rock.

And that's where we consider its height
and weight, and our task to lift it or not.

Resurrection Shuffle

Worlebury Camp
appears on all the maps
overlooking the town

pleased as Lazarus.
Buried beneath its base
prospectors found

tidy crushed skulls
leaf-shaped arrowheads
sling-stones and spindle whorls

flint tools for eating
the odd woolly mammoth.
Local luminaries,

much enamoured
by myth and yore, their kinship
with prudence and thrift,

paid tree-fellers
to unveil arresting
grain storage pits;

lean and hungry quarrymen
to blast for silver galena
and soothing calamine;

stone-faced builders
to creep up the hill
with colonnades and windows.

The damage caused
such threat to their regard
they hatched the perfect patsies—

small boys
in summer holidays
who rolled away stones.

Gymnast

The sight of her on the floor
at the schools' county championships
made my thighs tighten, lashed my muscles
together. It was cool to see other boys
look at her. It was like she could feel
their eyes resting on her skin.

She said let's run into the sea
at nightfall, stay there till morning,
but the farther we went to look for it,
the thicker the estuary's mud.
We spent the night in the sand dunes
with whisky and menthol cigarettes.

One Saturday she took me shoplifting.
Postcards, thimbles, a box of fudge;
three metres of fabric for dressmaking.
On the way home she gave me a blowjob
in her father's allotment while four old men
drank mugs of tea in a neighbouring hut.

She asked if I would like to watch her dance
naked in public places. We borrowed
a ghetto blaster and disco tape,
funked it up and down outside the Town Hall,
behind the auctioneers, against a wall
until a quarter past fairy gold.

She asked if I would like to watch her
having sex with her best friend.
She gave me a cheesecloth cushion to sit on
and hid me in her wardrobe to watch the show.
One day, the last day, I hid again,
to surprise her, to jump out at her,

and watched as she fell face down on the floor,
her father inside her, where he remained
until he finished. She laid still for eight minutes,
straightened her clothes and left.
I don't know if she saw me watching—
I think she saw me watching.

Walking in Woods

I remember your asthma—
I'd never met a boy who wheezed,
or seen an inhaler; you whispered,
squirting secrets into your lungs.

I remember your scrambler—
its shrieking whine and rush of air,
holes burned through my trousers,
two boys of nine on motorbikes.

I remember your room—
playing with our willies while mums and dads
drank sherry in the lounge; fifties' men yearning
for licentious sixties' women.

I remember your sister—
she wore jodhpurs, rode horses,
wiped fine blonde hair from her forehead,
gave me my first erection. I loved her.

I remember woods near your house—
textbook campaigns, swinging by ropes:
the Monmouth Rebellion; Little Big Horn.
So many men falling with bloody hilarity.

I did not see the black thoughts—
how they were sown, sprouted roots,
harrowed the wild woodland playground
to this place of unadorned silence.

I remember, before the thunder,
a clear sky, a cool boy, racing.

French Lessons

Old Ernie scratches present tense conjugations
on the blackboard with his long white finger.
Archie stops his ears while Billy winces and whistles.

Elaine smiles and sucks her pencil at the same time,
which seems a very French thing to do,
though she does it in Art and Chemistry too.

Once we had to sit together for a talk
about the most abundant compound on Earth,
how all life depends on universal solvent,

begins in nascent, beating, liquid phase,
moves to hard maturing solid state,
then drifts away, drowsy, gaseous, content.

Elaine says there is another universal solvent
with the power to dissolve everything,
turn base metal into gold, make us immortal.

Archie overhears us and stops his ears,
Billy winces and whistles, on the blackboard
Ernie grinds the perfect unconditional future *amour*.

The Gull in the Dunes

This is no way to carry on, it cries.
Lying here with your Player's No.6
a punnet of strawberries and Mick
Naismith's girlfriend. Shame on you.

It's true, Mick Naismith's girlfriend is eager
to learn how the resulting erosion
of silicon dioxide provides meagre
purchase for feet, knees, elbows and bottoms.

But please, take your hand from inside her knickers,
her bra off your head, get straight back to school.
You're missing double RE and the story
of the fig trees that summer too soon.

Young Samoans on Tour

They arrived crashing from the coach
looking like the road crew from Judas Priest;
their smoky scent unleashed
a loosening of our bowels.

Of course, we laughed at them—
woven with tattoos, slapping flanks, releasing
their Manu, poking out their tongues—
but we were scared shitless.

When the snow began to fall they said
the sky was dying, heaven was making
its way to hell, the soft white rain
was the devil's feet.

After the game, as we nursed our fractures,
someone explained to them the principles
of precipitation, how free it is
from prediction,

that even in Space, on peaks
of wintering moons, crystal water gathers
in sky-formed heavy metal
showing no possibility of pain.

The Gas Hearted Student

It makes so little sense, says Kenny
in the library. He is reading Tzara
and his face begins to beat.

He suggests we juggle Rubik's cubes.
We go to the pub instead: locals throw police
dogs into the street with their throats cut.

After more pork scratchings Kenny starts
to feel stupid and begins to cry.
We go back to our flat and eight hours later

I wake up staring at his cock, which is excited
to see me at this time of day, more so
than I to see it in such a state.

I ask him to respect my desires,
and he does. We have sausages for breakfast.
Kenny plays with his grilled tomatoes.

This evening, in our seats at the theatre,
Mouth, Nose, Ear and friends
enter Kenny's mind in flippers and goggles

handing out advice about the tipping
over of bins while the neighbours sleep.
One is dressed as a transgendered Che Guevara

and waves fresh offal at the audience.
Kenny has a little French and asks them to stop,
but they are insistent and not even Romanian.

One wears a Kurt Cobain mask and wig
and pushes a pram filled with scrap metal.
There is frottage, and it is not simulated.

Kenny shouts: *You're nothing but a tribute band!*
Away and play my rusty trombone! as if it's an insult.
He grabs my hand, pulls me through the fire door
out into the street and we disappear like traffic.

Rome

columns of marble
cream-coloured fangs
grow like culture
in a Petri dish.
One, its legend

M
V
S
S
O
L
I
N
I

D
V
X

cleaned daily

Eating Bear Claws

We meet in a bar, corner of Washington.
He's the size of the Lincoln Memorial

but less white. People wonder if they saw
him once play nose tackle for the Redskins.

He drinks peach schnapps, eats a pile of Bear Claws.
I buy him a beer. We order pizza.

He has a plan. 'You ain't gotta hit 'em.
You ain't gotta shoot 'em. You just gotta

confuse 'em.' We hammer home a bottle
of Tequila, he mounts the table, throws

half-finished pastries at the ceiling fan,
spreading his love and largesse through the room.

It clears the floor. He sings Curly McLain
numbers. I slip on tap shoes to applause

before the barman asks us to leave.
Coated with sugar, we slip-slide onto

snow-sifted streets, wish ourselves the longest lives,
embracing every sweet madness on offer.

Jewish Quarter, Prague

they buried the dead
on top of one another
due to restricted space

and the ground rose

they stopped
not because they ran
out of bodies

but feared the rising mountain
would call itself Zion
and kick down its doors

Addis Ababa

The sky at night
a black sheet

with a string
of bright bullet holes

through which an eye
blinks

Catalonia

From our terrace, we see the sun schlep
behind hills in the west like a throbbing giant
naranja undressing for bed.

On the table, a torn and dirty tourist
leaflet speaks of thirsty mountain trails
through which some famous people fled,

or were stopped, or on which they slept,
or were caught and returned, or hollowed out
their simple tunnels of thought

while waiting for their narrow gates to open
beside the wide and tideless Mediterranean.
Next door, a neighbour cries and breaks a glass.

Across the harbour, a brass band tunes up.
In the square, boys argue over a ball.
Below, a cat yowls to be mated.

In the northward sweep of slow-moving mist,
terracotta tiles wave like idle fists
and starlings perform evensong ballet.

Red Light Through a Blizzard

for Carol Farrelly

Falling through the night

fragments of heaven.

Beyond the depression

of land

you see

a heart beating.

You turn to me

palms up

coat open

like wings.

Roadside

So, you like musicals? he said,
the flat tyre collapsing his car
like a poorly wrought soufflé.

And cooking, I said, knowing
where he was going.

Reformation

Luther, she says when we search for something
to watch on the telly.
I say I'm not really interested
in another film about Henry VIII.

No, she says, switching channel
to the BBC
and the massive attack
of Idris Elba's shadow.

Oh, I see, I say,
noticing how she prepares
for this thrilling scripture
with red wine and pretzels.

As I watch I think
what guy wouldn't want to be
Idris Elba?
Just to have his name,

his stride, his sigh.
He is one of the ten
hottest men on the planet,
she says, nailing her thesis

to the door of my heart.
I prefer the perfect
trochee of his name, I say,
as she wipes salt from her lips.

Are you jealous? she says.
That's just silly. He's a story.
Like Harry Potter. Like Jesus.
He's not real, like you.

Threshold

As an act of love
I promise to have
A crimson tattoo
Of little red hearts
In the softened wheals
Your teeth left behind.

Love Often Bares its Teeth

I am waiting for the number 44 bus,
it is raining and my bag is full of books
I have become less than keen to read;
they weigh me down, prod and bump
as if I carry a badly-concealed family
of cats. And not for the first time.

When I board I notice you are the driver—
I don't know whether to make some remark,
don't want to belittle your new occupation,
can't decide if I should comment on how well
you fill the uniform, if this might be
inappropriate. And not for the first time.

I pay my fare, give you a tip
because I don't have the right change,
sit in my favourite seat, enjoy the sting
and blind of oncoming traffic, see your face
on the front page of the Metro
with the story of your dimples. And, damn it,

the elderly man sitting by the window,
who swats the rain as it hits the glass,
growls curses or compliments—
it's difficult to tell them apart, especially at night—
is also you. Your unshaven face is no disguise,
nor the smell of piss and chips, lager

and Hilary Duff's 'With Love'. Strangely,
you are also changing a flat tyre
outside the Spar by the school. I recognise
your scarf, the angle at which you hold your head.
That coat will have to go to the dry cleaners,
with the soiled hanky you use on the jack.

On the top deck a fight erupts. I hear your voice,
its gentle pace, the peacemaker's tone,
and all goes quiet, the tempest quelled.
As I get off in Sauchiehall Street, you
get on with a surfboard, talking on your mobile
to your mother in New Zealand, whom you love,

and who loves you, of course, that's what mothers do,
and I swear you see me, nod, pay your fare,
go upstairs out of sight. The doors close.
As the bus pulls away water drips from my hair
down my back, inside my trousers. Even the rain
is you, breathing, beckoning, open-mouthed.

Clear Night on the M74

The journey is incurably long.
I know that before setting out.
It never changes,

though a fox in the under-carriage
can make it longer.
Journeys have their special

relativities.
Some end in relief,
others in catastrophe,

many in dazed familiarity –
it depends on the light,
the energy, the weather,

the station's playlist,
a lack of sugar,
the dreams at the wheel.

To remember a journey
it must have more
than uneaten sausage rolls

under the seat,
flames from the boot,
ice on the tyres.

The woman on the radio
said it was raining in Lancashire
the night we parted.

Outside the Playhouse

it is good
to see Greg

he lives
in Berlin

these days
so long

since we stole
jeans

from clotheslines
in St Ives

before the snow
began

to follow him
and he stopped

recognising
me

In My Mother's Garden

Badgers rake and rupture
claw the spruced up sward
like drunks.

White stripes tremble and tunnel,
lardy grey bodies quarry and quiver,
big fat arses wobble in delight,
scoring a grub-seeking nocturne.

But she induced a change
of nature. Installed
                        a motion light
to stun, overcome; leave them feeling
butt-badger naked; whispered stories
of badger-feasting during the war;
reminded them they were gassed
                        like her ancestors.

Now she offers covenants of peace:
peanut butter sandwiches,
a gift they honour.

Disinhibition in Aisle 32

You're never quite sure when they will come,
those moments, but you know when they're abroad,
like sounds you once heard on winds and wires,
scrapings on doorsteps, the stinging sweats

on your forehead. You prepare for it
as best you can: reading some of the books,
watching the news, going to the movies
(it's all the rage, you hear, without irony),
and listening, above all listening.

But there is nothing in your homemade bag
of insights that provides a strategy
to cope when your father drops his drawers
in Oils and Dressings at Tesco and weeps
oh god, not another year of wanking.

The Headaches Are Back

They are like that couple we used to know
when we lived near Great Yarmouth,
the ones who borrowed the steam stripper
and wore those matching blue berets.

If I recall correctly the husband
was named Les and his wife was Billy
though it could have been the other way round:
they were the perfect interchangeable couple.

She made flat and tasteless madeleines –
I think it was the absence of almond –
and Les laid carpets all over the village,
even at the bus stop and on the church roof.

I can hear their voices over the white noise,
through the steam, and they never return the stripper.

Edradour

for Rachel

Lay down a draft
watch it strengthen   colour

Offer up a body
reduce   to almost nothing

Lay down a word
its sweet   running water

Offer up a life
and its remains   your share

The Widow Resolves To Eat Chocolate Forever

How you refuse to moderate the number
of coals you put on the fire nightly

saying you will spend what money you have
on anything you want, like Oreos,

or fish you won't eat but rather eyeball
on the middle shelf of the cooler—

the way its mouth gapes, about to speak,
but rests, content to smile, scales aglow—

how you stare out the searing night grate
in a child's game, each of you determined

not to blink first, not to count days, but
to dazzle and be blind to winter.

One Way Ticket Round the World

All you need is an umbrella—
   because you must visit Scotland;

a reasonable camera—
   you don't want arguments, it's a long trip;

six small stones—
   you may happen upon a game of cricket;

a working knowledge of several creation myths—
   South Carolina differs only slightly from Tehran,
   Pretoria, and Glyndebourne;

endless bottles of Absinthe, a baguette, some chorizo—
   a nice salami will substitute – try one from Milan;

memories of astonishing sex—
   nights are often long, dark and cold;

a resistance to truth, a tolerance of jail-time—
   the Absinthe will help in this regard;

a fake moustache—
   days are often long, dark and cold;

an aptitude for seeing trees
   where there are none.

If you have never experienced astonishing sex,
   better-than-average sex will suffice.

While you're away, you can start a blog—
   but remember to take tissues;

under no circumstance refer to Dante, Swift or Odyssey—
   people throw stones for less.

If you weaken, and return, nobody will shake your hand—
   but don't let that stop you.